VALIANT WARRIOR

You have a mighty Father warring with you-

Nicole Bishop

VALIANT WARRIOR

HULU PUBLISHERS
ISBN 978-1-365-90109-6

VALIANT WARRIOR

DEDICATION & ACKNOWLEDGMENTS

This book is dedicated to my husband Gus. A mighty warrior for The Father's love. He wars in the love of Jesus and seeks to redeem the lost with the love of Jesus. He is strong because he knows where his strength comes from, The Lord. I am so blessed to be married to such a pillar of strength, courage, honor and humility. Thank you for being such a valiant warrior for The Lord and for all His sons.

I would also like to dedicate this book so my son Bailey. He has the heart of a lion and is also such a compassionate and caring person. I am very blessed to have a son with such a heart for others & The Lord.

Lastly, I would like to thank my husband, Gus who has lead our family well as a son of God. Thank you for leading by example in all that you do. Thank you for writing the forward and for loving like Christ loves us.

VALIANT WARRIOR

FOREWARD-By Gus Bishop

Who am I? Am I enough? Will I succeed? Will I make a good boyfriend and husband? Will I be a good father? Will I become the man I need to be? What kind of man am I? For that matter, what kind of man do I even want to be? These are the questions that most boys, young men and even older men are constantly asking ourselves. The majority of our lives, we will hear so many different voices telling us their answers to these questions for us. So many voices telling us who we are and who we should be and how we should respond and act to what the world throws at us.

In order for any of these questions to be answered with the truth, we must have a greater understanding of the One who speaks the truth. We must listen to the voice of our loving Heavenly Dad. We must begin to understand who He is and who He says we are. His voice sometimes speaks sternly with love but He is always calling us to a better place. His voice is always the truth. His voice calls us up not down. He wants us to understand that as His sons, we can view ourselves differently than the world tells us. Who we are and who we will be is what His focus is for us. Once we are in Christ, He no longer holds our past as our identity. Our identity as His son allows us to live with joy, peace, power and love knowing that we have a Dad who is always with us. He wants more for our lives than we could ever dream of.

This book is written in such a beautiful and power way that we get a glimpse of Dad's goodness and the way He see us- His sons. The words on the following pages gives a glimpse of His goodness, His love and thoughts of us. They inspire us to listen and believe not only about who He says He is, but also who He says we are. IN Him and because of what Jesus has accomplished, we can love Him freely and love others the way we love ourselves. In order to love others the way He does, we have to learn to love ourselves the way He loves us. Only from the inflow of His thoughts and love for us can we begin to love others as He does. Only from hearing and seeing ourselves the way He does can we love ourselves as His sons; mighty men, as strong and gentle warriors that accomplish all things to bring Him glory. This book gives us a glimpse at His thoughts about His sons.

VALIANT WARRIOR

INTRODUCTION

My name is Nicole, although I'm a woman The Lord spoke to me on your behalf- all the Valiant Warriors. For over a year, The Lord filled the pages of my journal with this book for you. These pages are His words He spoke to me for you. These pages are His heart for you, a new mindset He wants you to live from and identity He is calling you to as son.

This book was written to the sons of valor who have been enlisted in the battle for the Kingdom of Heaven on earth. The Father wants you to understand **your role in this life, your calling and also your identity as Son**. I hope you will seek the love of Jesus and walk with Him like never before.

To understand what Jesus is saying to you in this book, you must understand His identity. He is part of The Holy Trinity. The Trinity is the triune nature of God- three persons in One. God The Father, Jesus the Son and Holy Spirit. They comprise one God in three persons. At first, when I became a believer, I pictured a triangle, with God at the top "in charge" and Jesus and Holy Spirit as His "helpers." They are not His helpers, but part of His complex nature as three persons in one. It's hard for our human minds to grasp, just know that there are three people that comprise who God is.

Throughout this book, The Lord is speaking to you from each of these people that make Him God. He may also refer to "US" at times; just remember He's talking about all three of them- the trinity that makes Him God. Never knew this about God? Not sure He's three in one? Check out Genesis 1:26. "Then God said, "Let US make mankind in OUR image, in OUR likeness…"

Other times He speaks as "The I Am." There are many references in both the Old & New Testament that refer to God & Jesus as The I Am. He is all sufficient, there's nothing lacking- He is "The I AM." All the words He spoke to me on your behalf are in quotes. There's space on the pages to journal back to Him. Are you ready? Be excited. His words to you begin on page 6.

Thanks after
Nicee

VALIANT WARRIOR

"Faithful Son-

I begin these words, calling you to a new depth of love. My love is stronger than any earthly hurt or wound. Here in this place, I AM Father and friend. You are strong, but I AM stronger. If you allow Me to, you can rest in My strength. The flesh will try and tell you that doing things in My strength or asking for My help is weakness. There is nothing about wisdom that is weak. It is wise to rely on The Good Father who knows all and is all you will ever need."

"I Am not afraid of what you seek. Dare to ask the imaginable. Do you think I am intimidated by your "big" ask? I spoke the universe with billions of galaxies into existence and it had to obey at My command. Now, what is your big ask? What do you want Me to provide for you that you have fought for and its time for Me to take over? You must first come with a pure, repentant heart. Are their things you've hidden deep within your heart that keep Me from you? Are there sinful thoughts and desires that you have tolerated and minimized as though they were ok? If you want all that I Am fighting for your behalf, you must first remove the things that are not of Me that separate us."

"Where do you go in your imagination?"

"Who do you choose not to forgive?"

"These are sinful pride filled lies the enemy has allowed you to believe I will overlook and allow. I Am all that is pure. I cannot allow sin in My dwelling place. The more you are willing to admit and then ask for forgiveness the closer I Am able to be to you."

VALIANT WARRIOR

"Do you have a heart for Me, really? Are you going through the motions as the "man" everyone thinks you should be? Do you know yourself, the way I know you? Do you fear the young boy will come out if you let Me in? There's nothing wrong with coming to Me as My son- that is not weakness. That is trust and vulnerability, which gives you access to The Father's love."

"For many years you have had to fight. For many years you have held it together and your body and mind show it. I'm making a plea that you realize I want to carry your burdens and fight your battles."

"My battle is for the lost, alone, abandoned, afraid, the weak, the angry, the drunk and the strung out. My heart is for all My sons to know Me as Father. When you let Me fight your battle, we are able to reach more sons with My love because the enemy no longer has your mind held captive to your battle. That is the greatest strength-establishing an army camp with those around you fighting the same battle, delegating to each of the captains and general then moving on knowing the battle is won."

"Are you that brave? Do you want the enemy to continually win the battle and gain ground in your mind, family and friends? Then join My army and let Me fight your battles. I Am stronger, there's no one like Me, I Am not afraid of any person or circumstance you will ever face."

"It's up to you to position Me as the commander of your battles. I will not take it unless you offer it. You are the CEO and general of your life, are you willing to clean out your junk, get real and let Me reign in your life?"

"The enemy will lie and say it's weak to not fight your battle, but if you know My Father's promises of what He spoke thousands of years ago, you will know that the enemy is spitting lies and venom from behind prison bars and only has his voice to fight with. He only has the power people give him in their lives. The good news is- I have already won. The enemy has been defeated and there's nothing too big or too small I don't want to win for you."

"Are you ready to go to battle and shut the enemy up in your life and in your circumstances? Are you willing to remove the things that separate us? The more you remove that is not of Me, the closer I Am able to be. What are you willing to give Me? There's no shame. I see the things you have hidden for so long. Give them to Me."

VALIANT WARRIOR

"You cannot be strong without Me. Your might and your will cannot carry you alone. My strength is stronger, wisdom is knowing to use My strength instead of falling for the lie that you are weak to rely on Me-that you are to do "your part." Your part is faith. Faith alone. Walk in it. Trust Me."

"When you have faith in Me, you seek Me first. Give Me your dreams, desires, struggles, battles, fears and even failures. Relying on Me is strength at full potential. There is none stronger. There is no one wiser. There is no one who is mightier than My right hand. Only until your faith out works your works of your flesh will you succeed. Are you ready to stop believing the lie? Are you ready to be strong in your weakness? Do you believe I Am good? Do you believe I Am for you?"

"Adam's pride in the garden of Eden kept Me from My son Adam. He had to be removed from My presence because he listened to the lie of the enemy and committed the first sin. Because there is no sin in Me, he had to be removed from the garden- My dwelling place. My dwelling place today is in the hearts of My sons and daughters. Today's pride-filled sin that man believes is that this world is only about *accomplishing things* in My name. It's prideful because you are doing it with a heart just to *accomplish* something. Love is what I have asked you *to do*. When you seek Me first, allow Me to love you as Father then My love will naturally flow out into the world. Pride blinds the eyes of those who are lost. Pride even blinds the eyes of those who know Me. Pride keeps you reliant upon your works and not My Word. I spoke the world into existence; none is stronger. I created all things to glorify My Father. Can you stop long enough to let this sink in and stop believing the lie of pride?"

VALIANT WARRIOR

"What is pride?
> Your works.
> Your unwillingness to seek Me in all you do.
> Your lack of faith for the future that I have promised you.
> Your thought that you provide."

"I alone Am good. Blessings naturally flow from Me, when you seek My face and seek My strength- nothing makes you stronger. Faith in My strength is unmatched."

"Do you have that much faith? How well do you really <u>know</u> Me? Do you know *of* Me or do you know Me as some distant entity in the galaxies somewhere-disconnected from you and not aware of your current situation or your desires before you ask?"

"Maybe you see Me as a cruel tyrant who rules those who come against Me or some mean governor who only wants revenge. Maybe you don't think of Me at all and you don't even believe I really exist-you have only been a puppet going through the motions to get your way. Maybe you know Me well. There's so much more of Me I want you to know about Me. Do you care? Do you want to know Me? Do you have the faith to believe it when I share details about Me?"

"I alone Am:

> Good
> Eternal
> Love
> Peace
> Enduring
> Everlasting

I Am The Alpha and The Omega. I have always existed. There is none like Me. My heart is pure; My sole purpose is to glorify The Father. In Me there is hope, peace and love."

VALIANT WARRIOR

"How long must I call your name before you will listen?
Is it really strange that I would speak to you? Why wouldn't I? I love you and am calling your name. If you feel ashamed to be in My presence – lets do something about that- seek My face instead of My hand."

"What do you need to confess? Are you full of pride hidden in the form of jealousy, rage, resentment or fear? Those things are not of Me. When your flesh is consumed by things of this world, it dulls your sense to hear My voice. Then it keeps you away from Me in guilt and shame. Lets remove all the things that are not of Me."

"How's your thought life? What do you think about? Yourself? Your achievements or failures? My creation- the opposite sex in an inappropriate way? If you are not married, you are walking on another man's future covenant. Honor her in your mind and honor his future covenant and wife. I will provide for you the desires of your heart, but they must be pure and not out of lust of the flesh."

"What about the lie you choose to believe that you are never enough? Are you ready to quit celebrating at the pity party and realize all things are possible through Me? Are you willing to call yourself weak in humility- understanding that your "strength" is pride and that I Am your strength? Relying on My strength is not weakness it's wisdom. Few are willing to be wise because they are looking for affirmation from man. I Am not man. I formed man from dust. If you think affirmation from dust is strength you are a fool. Dust created nothing. I created all things from nothing. It's time to decide- do you care how dust views you or how I view you?"

VALIANT WARRIOR

"Dust Says:	I Say:
Things you possess define you.	I Am your Father.
Titles and achievements impress Me.	I Am your strength.
Wealth= success.	I Am near.
Fighting for your fame & honor makes you brave and strong.	I will never fail you or Forsake you."

"Seek to glorify My Father and I will handle all the rest. Your flesh can be overcome, but you need My strength to do it. In your heart, there's a garden where things grow. Fleshly seeds & seeds I sow. This place has many triggers to try and resurrect your fleshly desires. Will you choose to water the seed that sprouts up that is of the flesh or will you realize it's deception and pull it out from your garden of your heart before it can entangle, confuse, and distract you from your calling?"

"These seeds of the flesh feel good. They look like they are harmless and could be ok to just let them be for a while…. feel good for just a little bit longer. But the problem with this seed of deception is that it sends out runners into your mind that causes guilt, shame, resentment, and even doubt to pop up in other places. Vines that wrap around your neck and cause you to be silenced because you are ashamed and don't feel worthy to speak on my behalf."

"You have to want to want Me more than you want to feel good or look good in the eyes of dust. Dust can give you fame, honor and glory on this earth. But giving My Father all the honor and glory is who you were created to be. You decide: fleshly seeds or honor The Father."

VALIANT WARRIOR

"There is no need to feel small. No matter your circumstance, ask for My strength and guidance and you will be fortified with My strength. My strength is not of this world. My strength pierces the hearts and minds of the enemy and foes in paths. Stature is not an issue when you count on My strength. Many who rely on their own stature and strength are actually weak and vulnerable because they are blinded by pride and false strength."

"True strength comes from understanding your role as My son. There's nothing of mine I have kept from you. Are you willing to walk into your inheritance and take what was freely given to you by My love? Pride makes you blind to the freedom of grace and the power of My love. My love crumbles false kingdoms, past failures, future regrets, and even wars- in kingdoms or homes."

"You decide. Do you want to accept My love at the deepest level? Will you give up your strength for Mine? Are you brave enough to surrender to My love? Full surrender takes complete trust in who I Am."

"Do you know the real Me? Not who you think I Am, but who you have heard and seen with your own eyes…The Father who has been calling you home from the beginning. The one who's not impressed with your selfish ambition to impress people of this world. The one who's not intimidated by your past, rage, fears or even sinful choices. There's nothing hidden from My sight. I love you. I will always love you. Period. No conditions."

"When you believe in Me and know by faith that I Am *THE I AM* and that I will not settle for less than all of you- I Am here. I Am willing to wait until you are ready to rest. Rest here in this strength that is love."

"Many come to Me seeking answers and wonder why I don't answer the way they think I should. You cannot understand all of My ways. I was not created; I have always existed and Am in need of nothing. I see all things, hear all things including the desires of people's hearts before it's spoken."

VALIANT WARRIOR

"So why do I go after you? Because you are My son. You were created to be in close fellowship with Me- to discuss all things with Me, like the best of friends. Sin entered this world and mankind had to leave My presence until I could repair the relationship with a final sacrifice for sin- My Son."

"My Son took on your sinful nature so you can, by faith again be in close fellowship with Me as friend. Not as someone to fear but a faithful confidant. A friend who never leaves for forsakes you."

"Which would you rather have?

This life's:	Fellowship with Me:
Striving	Rest in My strength
Fear & Anxiety	Peace & confidence because I
Anger & Hurt	Am good and have a wonderful plan
Despair & Rejection	for you.
	Forgiveness & Freedom
	Peace & Acceptance"

"All of these things are on the table. I give them to you freely. You can't be a person on the fence, trying to hold onto the things of this world AND have all the things I Am offering. You have to make a choice. Give Me your burdens and your dreams- nothing is too small or too big for Me."

"I know this is new and maybe a little strange- men don't admit they need anyone. Well the good news is – I Am not just anyone. I Am the I AM. I created all things by My Word. All things were created because I said so. Good choice choosing Me. I Am for you and no one loves you more."

VALIANT WARRIOR

"Some days seem full of despair as though I have left you. Just stop and listen. I haven't left you. I never leave your side never. Your feelings will feel different at times because they are <u>feelings</u>. I Am not feelings and Am not dependant upon circumstances. I Am eternal and unchanging and Am always good. I Am love. I created you so you could know it in the bones of your faith not in the emotions of feelings."

"Feelings can be dangerous. They can make you think things are uncertain when nothing has changed. You have to see through your eyes of faith and feel the breath I put in your lungs. When you feel alone, like hope is gone, take a deep breath and feel the breath I put in your lungs. I Am life. I haven't left you and never will."

VALIANT WARRIOR

Lord, I know you are good, but sometimes life doesn't seem fair. Children dying of cancer, hopeless ones who don't want to know you, the angry and the addicted, the spiteful and outright vengeful. How can we sit by and watch as though we can do nothing about it? I know you are good, powerful, but how do I deal with these things when they don't make sense and are hard to endure?

"Unfortunately, sickness and disease are a result of willful disobedience that occurred in the garden with Adam and Eve. The rippling effect from their decision has hurt many generations and will continue to hurt people to come. You can intercede on their behalf. Pray for those who persecute you. When this world says fight, I say love. When this world says give up hope, I say pray and trust. I Am good and that won't change. This world perverted My goodness- seek Me; hear Me speak so you can be *life* to the broken."

"Not all those who are sick are healed in the body on earth. Some are meant to be restored with Me. Value the time you have been given. Value those I have placed in your families. Those who have called you family-genealogy is irrelevant. Are you welcoming the broken and the lost into your family? Who needs a father that doesn't know Me? Who needs a brother that you can strengthen? You are equipped to be that for them because you choose to rely on Me for all things- big or small. Intercede for those who persecute you. They need Me most because they are hurt and blinded by pride to the point of thinking they don't need Me. You can call them back to Me. Pray for their hearts to long to know Me, that they would realize they need Me and the hurt they feel that appears as bitterness, hurt and even anger is the lost fellowship with Me that they need to repent from."

"Pray on behalf of the broken and the lost. Pray for opportunities to speak life into people- no matter where you are or who it might be- everyone wants to know My love for them. Be of good courage- I will give you the words when the time is right if your heart is willing. Pray. Open your mouth and I will handle the rest."

VALIANT WARRIOR

"Seek My will above the things of this world. Seek My face and not My hand. You are a world changer if you are willing to fight My battle. My sons are out there- some are on the wrong side of the field. The war is won by love. Not by pride and force but by faith in Me, prayer and words of My love for them. Sit up – it's time for battle."

"Freedom was bought by My love. My love was shown in My Son's face and what He did on the cross on your behalf. Freedom was not free and it's not free today. Freedom was bought with a price. My Son paid for your freedom, now it's time you walk in it. This purchase was not out of guilt, resentment or shame for your sins; this purchase was to bring you back to Me so we could be friends."

"Guilt and shame are not of Me. When you hear condemning thoughts or feel ashamed, know that is from the father of lies and not Me. I Am The Good Father, who calls you up higher not because I'm embarrassed but because I have called you to a place of honor; seated beside Me at My banquet table. This is My Father's table. All His sons and daughters have a seat reserved here. This is a never ending feast, full of joy, happiness and acceptance because there's no guilt, shame, regret, or condemnation only Our presence and complete love that surrounds all who are gathered. You are welcome here; you don't even have to ask. This seat has been reserved for you since you accepted Me by faith. You can't loose this seat; it's reserved for you alone. You don't loose your seat when you run from Me; commit sins of the flesh or in the mind. My love never fails and is unconditional."

"When you transgress against My will you must confess those sins. Those sins are not welcome here with Us. When you give them to Me in prayers of confession they are no more. The enemy has nothing to stand on because the memory of those things are no longer existent in My sight. Your eyes of faith and hearing of My love for you is how you know are welcome in this place. I Am here to love and honor you as My son, not condemn you."

VALIANT WARRIOR

"Deny the enemy any ammunition and give Me the things he has tormented you with for so long. Look to the East, what do you see? My promise fulfilled. It is a new day, just like I said it would be. You cannot hold onto the regrets of the past. Today is new. Let My peace, hope, and joy restore the things I have planted deep within your heart. My love has watered this seed for a long time now it's time to allow it to take root in your life. Don't fear the new beginning. Don't listen to the liar pointing out past mistakes. What I plant, I will nourish and provide for you. My promise never fails. Believe in Me. Hope is on the way. Dare to dream again. Sit at the table and look at all My sons and daughters here. This place is full of laughter and joy. There is no sorrow, worry or fear. I Am in control when you let Me. Are you willing to let Me cultivate the soil and allow the seeds I planted come alive in you?"

VALIANT WARRIOR

"Some of you don't feel worthy to be called son. This is because your earthly father failed you. He was created out of dust and had a weak flesh. I was never created, always existed and have already won. I have never been weak and I call you son. <u>I</u> <u>AM</u> your qualifier. Forgive the man who was too weak in his flesh to love you the way you deserved to be loved and honored as son. I redeemed you from this hurt. I Am calling you out from the shadows. I Am proud to call you son and want you to sit with Me here in this place. Come home son."

VALIANT WARRIOR

"There are some of you who are fathers, fathers of your own sons. How's your patience? How's your presence? How's your forgiveness and love? Can they see My heart in your eyes and in the tone of your voice? Are you setting the example of strength, grace and truth that I model for you? If they see My strength in your eyes, they will want My strength too. The calling on your life as father is not meant to be taken lightly. This is a huge responsibility as well as an honor. Come up higher in the areas you are weak. I have given you all the tools you need to lay down those strongholds and carve a path for your future generations. This is your legacy- My love."

VALIANT WARRIOR

"Be of good courage and of strong faith, I Am fighting on your behalf. Although your earthly eyes may not see that I Am working, your spiritual eyes- eyes of faith can. Do you trust Me? Do you know that I Am good? Know that I Am working to make all things new, but you have to have the faith to believe it. Ask to use your eyes of faith/spiritual eyes to see My workings- you will be of good cheer because I Am working and you will see it with the eyes I give you. Eyes of the flesh cannot see My ways because they are prideful and fearful and look for things of potential danger rather than My blessings."

"I asked you in My Word to think and meditate on the things that are good. Use the eyes I gave you and with the mind of faith- this world becomes new for you because you are seeing it filled with hope, joy and peace; that everything is going to be ok- no matter what your fleshly eyes see."

"The fleshly earthly eyes have been tainted by regret, hurt, shame, anger and even resentfulness. My eyes of faith I give you only see My goodness, which always leads to joy and peace."

"Would you rather have joy and peace or feel like you are "fighting" for yourself and protecting yourself from future hurt by choosing to see your life with earthly eyes or would you rather choose to know I Am fighting for you and no weapon formed against you will prosper; and that I Am making all things new?

<u>Spiritual Eyes:</u>
Eyes of faith
The victorious one's dwelling place.
See things that are yet to be.
See things that draw you to Me.
See things I Am making new.

<u>Fleshly Eyes:</u>
Eyes of the earth
The defeated one's dwelling place.
Fear things that could happen=dread & fear.
See things as a threat & draw you to self -preservation."

VALIANT WARRIOR

"It takes faith and a choice to use the eyes of faith I freely give you. If you don't have faith, they can't operate and you will revert back to your earthly eyes."

"Do you have the faith?
  -Can you trust Me if I go silent?
  -Do you believe I will never leave your side, even if you can't hear Me?
  -Do you know I Am fighting on your behalf in areas you haven't even asked for help with yet?
  -Do you trust Me that all things work out for good for those who trust in Me? Even when they hurt and you don't see the "why" behind what happened?
  -Can you let go of your fight and walk along side Me and draw from My strength through the power of your faith I gave you?
  -Can you seek Me even in times of hurt flesh instead of lashing out in weakness?"

"When you use the eyes I gave you through faith and obedience, the things of this world no longer seem like a threat. They never really were. It's the power you choose to give away and not *actual* power that came from the enemy or the circumstance. The enemy can only be given power by those who give it to him."

"Use My strength to ignore his tactics. Yes, things in your life are hard at times, even painful but it can be manageable if you don't allow difficult things to take root and dwell in your heart. They are like weeds in a garden. They seem like mere annoyances at first, but before you know it they grow and develop a deep root system. By the time you realize that this thought pattern or behavior is no longer welcome in My dwelling place of your heart -you go to pull but the root system has grown so much it takes out other things with it and leaves a huge hole in your garden of your heart. The hole was caused by the root system of regret and shame, and pride of trying to protect yourself from it happening again."

VALIANT WARRIOR

"But that's the serpent speaking to you in the garden. When the seeds of <u>weeds</u> drift into your garden of your heart, be alert and realize their voice. They are not welcome here and you need to remove them before they have a chance to sprout. When you are in close fellowship with Me and know My voice and walk with Me daily in My garden- going over the condition of your heart with Me, I can gently show you the seeds that are weeds before they have a chance to harm you and we will remove them together. There's nothing to fear because I will show you them if you allow Me to teach you what has to go."

"Some things in your heart's garden you love and they are not good for you. I have told you they don't belong but you are allowing them to reside with Us. I Am not a God that compromises. I Am Good and Holy. I cannot allow you to defile My dwelling place. Are you ready to allow Me to plow your heart's garden? When we plow it we are starting over. This will provide a perfect condition of your heart by removing the things that were rooted in fear and allow the seeds I planted in you to grow by faith. I cannot plow your garden of your heart without your permission. There's even pride regarding some the sinful things here. You know they don't belong but yet secretly you choose to adore them. I will wait until you are ready."

"When you are ready, show Me the things that don't belong by confessing their former importance in your life- who do you refuse to forgive? That's a full-grown tree here in the garden that has matured and now producing fruit with evil seeds of hate and resentment to tarnish the good soil here."

"How's your thought life? Is it honoring Me? Walk with Me in the garden of your heart, we will go together and till up this place and start over. I will help you see other things you might have tolerated in your heart that no longer are welcome. Walk with Me and lets go to work."

VALIANT WARRIOR

"My people rebel against Me for their own gain. My Son left the message "love your neighbor as yourself" but yet even this generation has yet to obey. The love of pride and the will to be "right" has out manned the love I require. Until My people —all people learn to truly love others, as themselves there will always be war. War for possessions, power and pride. Look at the Roman Empire- their emperors called themselves gods. Where are their great cities and statues now? In ruins. Idolatry is pride, pride is rebellion against love. Why must someone always be "right?" What if you choose what is truly right- love? Unfortunately pride causes hatred and blindness, fear and resentment toward others. My hope for you is that you would let My love for you saturate the garden of your heart so the harvest that is produced causes a revolution of love. But that requires that you are still and that you listen to My voice crying in the wilderness of your heart."

"Can you put down your weapons you justify as "being right?" I didn't call you to fight <u>for</u> Me- I called you to love all people. It doesn't matter who they are: Arab, Hindi, drug dealers, prostitutes, hypocritical Christians- all of them. They are equal in My sight- My sons and daughters. Just because some choose not to accept My love doesn't make them any less *valuable* to Me. Love them <u>anyway</u>. Don't love from a place of pity that shows how "great" you are for loving sinners- that's a white washed tomb in My sight. Genuinely love them as they are. That is where My love is shown. That's how the water that is My grace and mercy makes its way from your hearts' garden and has the ability to open the eyes and ears of the lost through the Holy Spirit's work in them."

"It first starts with My love shown in your eyes. I know that some seem like they don't "deserve" your love or My love but remember when I told Paul... "All fall short of the glory of God?" That includes you. I died for you- no one <u>deserves</u> My love but I chose to freely give it so that you could choose to freely accept or reject it."

VALIANT WARRIOR

"Heart check:
Do you love yourself?
Do you love yourself to the point of idolatry?
Do you elevate yourself in a place of honor *on My throne?*
Do you love others as yourself?"

"You should love yourself because I love you. I have called you "son" by choice. I will never leave you or mislead you. You should be confident but not arrogant or prideful- just strong and confident because you recognize My grace that was extended to you and also where your strength comes from- Me."

"Loving others as yourself is not easy-It will take work, but I will be with you along the way. When "difficult" people try to make you angry, ask for My peace to overcome you so your heart becomes unaffected."

"Do you truly care about the lost? More than you care about being right? Don't fight to win an argument. Listen and be peaceful in the moment. Let the other person speak and respond back in love. When your heart is right I will cause <u>all</u> things to work for My glory. If your flesh makes you feel as though this is too passive and weak just look at The Roman Empire- in ruins. Pride always comes before the fall."

"The enemy will get louder because your have ignored his taunting, but that just proves My love is powerful. Smile and rejoice in the times of trial. I haven't forsaken you and the <u>war</u> has already been won. The mission of this war is about how many people can you point back to Me and My love."

VALIANT WARRIOR

"This life is full of distractions. Some created by others and some created by you. Until you carve out intentional time with Me, you will be impacted by these distractions. Is your longing to know Me more valuable to you? Are you going to choose anger or peace in the times of frustration? It's never going to be a perfect circumstance when you can plan on it- it will happen at inconvenient times, these are part of the trials and tribulations I spoke about. Distractions and frustrations come in many forms. They can be on your day off, on your way to church or even in the middle of the night. No matter when they come, they are not going to be easily ignored. This is where you strengthen your faith. You have to choose My love for you and My peace I granted you over frustration, anxiety or fear. You have to choose to be disciplined to seek Me out instead of your favorite distraction from Me. I'm not saying it should be out of obligation but out of the desire to be closer to Me as friend and Father who wants time with you."

VALIANT WARRIOR

"Young men open your eyes to what I am speaking. Many of you have the faith to get by; some of you think you will get by on your father's faith. That's not the way faith works. Faith has its own portion per person. You cannot have enough faith for someone else and you cannot get by on somone elses faith. Faith is a heart condition. How's your heart? Would you know if your faith is authentic? How can you tell? Do you trust Me when things aren't going your way?"

"Did you consider that <u>because</u> I Am good, these frustrating things could be steering you out of harms way or into a blessing? The flesh without faith throws temper tantrums and says: *"Where's God? I'm all alone, I can't hear Him- why can't I get my own way?"*

"Faith and character are tested when you don't get your way. Which would you prefer, your way or My way? Again, this goes back to your heart condition….do you believe I AM good? The fact that your faith might not be authentic enough to grasp it doesn't change the fact that I AM good. Faith is complete trust in Me, knowing that despite what your earthly eyes see, your circumstance or distractions aimed at you- you are at peace because you know I haven't left your side. You know I will never forsake you or lead you astray. Remember that I Am omniscient. I know all things. Remember that I Am omnipresent. I Am everywhere at once. I Am faithful to pursue. Are you there yet? Complete trust in Me despite what your flesh is telling you?"

"Have you allowed Me into your heart's dwelling place? Have you let your guard down to see Me for Me and not the empty words you sing from a screen? I need warriors not pretenders. Many of you walk around with a mask of pretention and everyone buys it <u>but</u> Me. Are you there for them or to know and worship Me?"

"It hurts when people use My house of worship for their gain. I know people just want to fit in and look impressive to those their age but that is a dead faith. I need men with faith for themselves, fire that burns deep inside despite your circumstance. Are you man enough to go against what you've been doing and let Me into your dwelling place of your heart?"

VALIANT WARRIOR

"I realize this is new to some and maybe even old news to others, but there's a reason I have brought you to these words-both ends of the spectrum need to hear this. Luke warm routines don't inspire Me or impress Me. Would you hold the same birthday party for your child year after year because it's a reliable routine you are comfortable with?"

"I didn't ask you to be comfortable. I asked you to let Me into your heart's garden. If you only contain Me to a place that you are comfortable with you don't have enough faith and don't trust Me unconditionally. Again, a heart issue."

"What are you afraid of? Man's impression of you? Did I send Jesus to tell you to be careful of what others think of you and to keep a routine? No. His message was the same one I have said from the beginning. I love you and I Am calling you to Love the Lord with all your heart, soul and strength."

"Doing the same thing doesn't take all your strength. It's actually a lack of faith because you control the outcome which ultimately is not allowing Me to lead you where I truly want to take you. Just like your child's birthday party is how I want you to approach your walk with Me-expectant. Wanting it to be the best it can be, believing that the sky is the limit, that you will hold nothing back to make the experience something great. Not holding the same party year after year, Sunday after Sunday expecting a new result. For those too young to have kids-think of your own party. How would it feel if someone you loved forgot your birthday? I endure this forgetfulness because I love you. What if you went to your party and it was the same as the last 16 years but now you are 30? You would feel a little hurt inside that people you loved didn't put more effort into it and maybe even feel upset with the fact they were ok with the same thing even though it was out-dated and no longer relevant to your stage in your life."

VALIANT WARRIOR

"What about the surprise party? Each year everyone approaching a birthday secretly hopes to get something special. A visit from friends, birthday wishes from people you haven't heard from in a while, time for fellowship and laughter- a place where you feel truly loved and adored. That's the expectancy I need you to place in your heart daily. Excitement, something great is going to happen today because you have faith in the One who called you because you would never dream that two days would ever be the same with Me in charge- the sky is the limit."

"Where do you want to go? Who do you want to be? Do you want to stay the same or become someone on fire with faith burning in their heart for all I Am willing to give? This takes faith and expectancy. Set time to know Me and My will for your life. Set time to seek Me and tear down the walls of your heart you have guarded for so long. I Am good. Once you truly relax and allow Me into those places things will change. Your faith will be authentic because you will have experienced Me for yourself and no one can take that from you."

"Go out each day seeking My face, My guidance expecting it to be a celebration. The birthday you are celebrating is authentic faith despite your feelings. Faith is time with Me. Hearing My voice and obeying Me when I ask you to go, speak or stay. Obeying Me when it might be awkward to a friend. Do you want the ways you've held onto for so long or are you ready to go where I want to take you with your new found faith?"

VALIANT WARRIOR

"Can you feel it? The peace within your heart? There's no striving required. This peace is from truly trusting in Me for all things. Your possessions, family, future, dreams and cares of this world. When you have authentic faith you will harvest My peace in your heart. You know that I Am near. You know that I Am making all things new. I Am never going to leave your side or leave you to destruction. You trust even when things appear out of control because you know I Am stronger and you have given Me the authority over your life to guide and protect you in the way I see fit. You trust My decisions because you have authentic faith and fellowship with Me. This is walking in the garden like Adam and Eve-fellowship with Me. I yearn to be trusted and honored enough to be sought after and obeyed. You have a great honor placed upon your life as a man- to lead others into this place."

VALIANT WARRIOR

"Faithful one-
Yet again you have shown up to hear My words I have for you. Seeking
Me is what I require, you have shown yourself faithful to the small things,
are you ready to grow in your trust in Me for the even bigger things?
It will seem like you are out of control, like being out in the ocean waves at
night. Scary, unsettling and vulnerable. But it's not real. It's a lie the
enemy has fooled so many into believing. When you are willing to
surrender yourself completely you are able to see that by giving Me control
you have the faith that's required for Me to work in your life and you are
in control by giving Me control. This sea is no longer frightening. I
control the wind, waves; nothing can come at you in the darkness of the
depth of the sea because My light illuminates what used to be darkness."

"The flesh says not to even put yourself in this circumstance because the
flesh works from the root of fear. I fear nothing- I Am not afraid. Are you
ready to no longer fear? Even if things are not going your way currently or
when troubles of this life start to surround you? Step out of the boat and
see what happens. Do you have the faith and courage it takes to
completely surrender your control to Me? When the waves come or
something starts to scare you because you can't control it- are you going to
retreat back to the boat or are you willing to call upon My name and tell
these lies to flee in My name? You will see just how fake these feelings
really are once you begin to laugh at the flesh and its attempts to cause you
to fear. Faith in My strength is Truth and My Truth is power. Seek Me,
My strength, and My name."

VALIANT WARRIOR

"Love is all around you. Love is not feminine- just a girl expression. Love is limitless patience and kindness toward an enemy or a stranger. Love knows no bounds. Love is not easy for most. It requires sacrifice of yourself to truly love someone who has mistreated you or who would consider you an enemy."

"Love takes strength and courage. This life has watered down the emotion to a physical state and to a "feminine" emotion that appears weak if spoken by a man. That is no My intention of love. Love is honor and courage to do what's right and to respond in love because The Father first loved you."

"Are you strong enough to change the culture of love? Can you lead the battle with a war cry of love? My love expressed through a man of valor breaks down walls and unites My people for The Father's plan of redemption. I love you and need your strength powered by The Father's love. This love breaks the silence of old wounds and will allow The Father's love to penetrate the pain and heal hurts to make people new again. This love removes hate and animosity. This love gives to others who according to this life don't "deserve" it. My Father's love is radical- there's nothing that can match it. Search the earth and dare to find something comparable. There is none."

"To renew your mind and learn how to love in power and not believe love is a weakness look at the evidence of what love has done: **John 12:19.**"

"Many accusers will come your way but nothing can match the Truth and power of The Father's love. The Pharisees thought they had won when I was crucified, but love won redemption for all mankind. This redemption is available to all despite The Father knowing *who* would reject it. Love is perfect because it doesn't demand anything in return or expect a certain outcome. Love is because The Father loved first. Are you bold enough to face your accusers and still choose love over retaliation?"

VALIANT WARRIOR

"John 19:21"
"The One who delivered them out of bondage and slavery, made them a nation and taught them how to love by worship and sacrifice was nailed to the cross. Pride puffs up many men to adorn themselves in titles and outfits that "dignify" themselves instead of magnifying The Father. Which will you choose- titles provided by earthly gain or the title that comes with obedience to The Father's love through faith- "Son.""

"Hebrews 1:1-11"
"I Am The I AM. The eternal One who came to save the least and the lost from eternal separation from The Father's love. There is none greater than this love. Dare to walk in this strength of The Father's love. Dare to reject the flesh's pleas of bitterness, rage and rejection and choose The Father's love shown by your actions instead."

"Difficult times will come and go. Are you willing to put the dead things to rest? When you continually dwell on things that are dead you stop moving toward the future." *What things are dead?*
"The past mistakes you made before you knew Me. The past things that broke your heart. The past things you thought would be one way but turned out to be completely different. You wander around in this graveyard of regret and there's no reason for Me to resurrect something that never should have flourished in your life to begin with. I make all things new. The past is the past. Give your present and your future to Me and stop dwelling on what could have been and focus on who I Am."

"Ask for forgiveness for the things you did that you haven't repented of and walk away- without looking back. No regrets, I make no mistakes. Do you believe in Me or in your efforts? Your efforts will always cause you to strive with empty results. My efforts never fail. Where most people fail is by never asking for My opinion, direction or permission. When you seek direction, guidance and permission from Me & rely on My strength, all things are possible and they are for the glory of The Father. So, they will not exhaust you, disappoint your or later cause regret because they result in love from The Father."

VALIANT WARRIOR

"What things do you hold onto from your past that have long ago passed away that we need to finally let go of together?

-Your earthly father's failures?
-Your dream to become wealthier than your father?
-Your desire to be the best in all that you do?
-Your regret for not seeking Me at a younger age?
-Your regret of not loving others that are no longer here on earth?
-The regret of choices that ended up in failure and pain?

All of those things can be made new. You need to give Me all of the dead things that have held you back and caused you to mourn for their loss or disappointment. You are no good to yourself, your family and those I've placed around you when you continually want to walk around in this graveyard of regret."

"It's time to heal. It's time to forgive. Who are you angry at? Me? Do you feel like I let you down and should have done something, or even warned you? Are you angry at yourself? Do you feel like you should have known better and can't seem to break this pattern of bad choices? Are you mad at someone else? List them out, one by one. Share with Me the things you have buried deep in your heart that have been allowed to cloud your mind:"

VALIANT WARRIOR

"It's time to get this out and make things new, I have so many things I need you to do, but this is part of what makes you pause and hesitate: fear of repeating past mistakes and fear "I will let you down again". Yell, rant and rave about these things if you need to, but lets get it out."

"The mourning clothes stop here, its time to return to battle in the armor I made for you and let go. I won't be angry at you for sharing how you feel about Me- why are you mad at Me? Why are you resentful of Me? What do you feel like I did or didn't do that got you to this place?"

"Who else has disappointed you?"

"What about yourself? Are you ready to forgive yourself?"

"All of these things, earthly, fleshly or even your feelings about Me are just feelings that the enemy has used to control your mind to keep you in the graveyard of regret. Some people like feeling sorry for themselves and feel like it's what they deserve-to dwell in this place of self-pity, regret and shame that live in this place. I make all things new. You are not alone, I never left you. I know it's new and hard to believe these things must end now, but you are going into battle and there's no time to drag dead things of the past with you and there's no time to go back and revisit the graveyard of regret. My love is strong enough to overcome your past mistakes. Give them to Me now- all of them:"

"My love is strong enough to forgive your frustration, anger and regrets of the past- give them to me now –all of them. Yes, even that one. The one you love to hate yourself for that you think you should have known better and choose to do it anyway. All of them:"

VALIANT WARRIOR

"It's My turn. Your past was not a mistake. You are not a mistake. I Am not ashamed of you, I Am not disappointed in you, I have not given up on you. My Words are truth and life and I cannot lie. I love you; I always have and always will. It's because of My love for you that we are moving from this place and not returning. I cannot take you where you are not willing to go. I Am patient & I will wait for you. Are you ready?"

"What are you scared of? Being afraid is not weak. Fear is not of Me, you have allowed the enemy to control your life through your mind via the tool of fear. There's nothing to fear when you walk with Me. No weapon formed against us will prosper. The difference is walking with Me and in My strength and knowing I Am for you and Am not disappointed in you and Am not embarrassed to walk with you. You are My son whom I love and want to walk this earth in love and power with to bring people to The Father. Do you want to be released from this past? To truly live? Hope, joy, peace and confidence that comes from the identity I gave you as My son."

"Here's your armor, you put it on when you are ready. I Am not going to rush you, but when you are ready to choose to only look ahead with the faith that I Am by your side and that fear and failure has already been defeated."

VALIANT WARRIOR

"Where's your faith? In the things you achieve or in the blessings you receive? Is it in Me, because of My righteousness I impart on you? Faith comes from trusting in the One who is faithful. This life is not always about gain, accomplishments and worth. This life is about the love of The Father and understanding His imparted righteousness on all those who believe. Do you believe because of the favor you have received or do you believe because of the feelings that prove My existence? Feelings may fail you, but I never will. You have to look beyond the feelings, things you fear, things that edify and things you desire. See beyond the gratification of success and look to The Father. There is no greater satisfaction. His presence, His grace, His mercy. His undivided attention on all who ask."

"Don't ask for things. Dare to ask to be. Are you willing to just be still and be in His presence for His presence sake? You are too busy in this life moving from goal to goal, project to project running from regrets of the past, making sure not to repeat the same "failures" that you are missing out on the more important portion of this life: relationship."

"Relationship doesn't go into circumstances with the mindset of what's in it for me. Relationship says- nothing else matters but the here and now in your presence. Do you trust Me enough to put the cares of this life on hold to just be with Me? To be in relationship for the sake of relationship?"

"True strength comes from knowing who I created you to be- in My presence. I created you for My Father's glory and when you seek to glorify yourself disguised as good deeds, it only breaks My heart because you truly don't understand The Father's love. He doesn't want you to do things, He wants all of you. Works were made dead when I arose from the dead."

"Open your eyes of faith and look around. What do you see? Can you see the broken, hurting, and the lost? Do you yearn for them to know Me the way you know Me? Why not? Nothing in it for you to gain? Selfishness is a form of pride. Self preservation prevents many from hearing My name and the love of The Father- this is not a guilt trip but just a statement about the weakness of man."

VALIANT WARRIOR

"Your weakness can be made strong if you rely on My strength and love others as you love yourself. What if that person were you? Would you want them to tell you about Me? Do you love yourself and your identity more you love others? The brief moment you sacrifice or even loose face by any rejection you receive doesn't matter in the years of eternity. Would you get over yourself for just one person to find Me?"

"Fellowship in The Father's presence is your qualifier. I have called you to bear witness to My existence and share the love of The Father. If you haven't experienced it for your sake you cannot share it with others because it is something you are still learning. The love of The Father is simple. He created you in Our image, to bear the image of Christ and to be love in the flesh so others believe. Love is not based upon your performance or how many souls you win, but based upon true love from The Father. He only requires faith. Is your faith based upon your experiences, circumstances, rewards you have received? Faith should not be conditional but because We loved you first, before We clothed you in righteousness."

"Be still and be with Me. You are not going to miss something if you are still and listen. A natural outpouring from sitting and being still is the peace and confidence of His presence in you wherever you go. You will naturally yearn for the lost to know this peace and love- it won't be a task to perform but out of the love The Father placed in your heart for the lost. Be still. Be with Me, know that I Am God."

"Do not put your fear of "failure" on Me. Your fear of failure is really a form of pride because you are trying to save face. Failure is not bad, who said that all things that don't go your way are a failure? Did you consider that it might be the correct outcome for the long-term solution I have planned? Failure is not trying, not being willing to be obedient and listen to My instruction. Failure is self-absorbed and not living for others. I Am always here for you but I cannot take things from you that are designed by nature to strengthen you."

VALIANT WARRIOR

"When you fail- loose something, miss out on something, disappoint or upset someone, it teaches you to be more diligent the next time, to plan and prepare or even more importantly be patient for My timing rather than trying to make something work I never asked you to do. When I call you to things, I will equip you for those things. But remember, seek Me first, My strength and glory for The Kingdom not yours."

"Honor. How well are you doing at honor? Do you honor your commitments? Do you honor your promises? Do you honor your body, mind and The Father? Honor is the deepest form of love because it sets feelings aside and allows the true nature of what should take place. It's not easy to honor a person who disrespects you. It's not easy to honor a commitment when it's no longer convenient. Its not easy honoring your body and mind because sinful thoughts and actions "seem" so harmless."

"When you dishonor yourself and others you are dishonoring The Father. He has clothed you in righteousness by My blood sacrifice and asks you to take up your cross and bare the weight and discomfort that comes by honoring others who "desire" revenge, who "deserve" neglect or backing out on a promise. When you dishonor yourself it is dishonoring My temple. Sinful acts and thoughts are never ok in My dwelling place. I dwell in you, so when you sin by actions or thoughts it's grieving My Spirit."

VALIANT WARRIOR

"Don't let this life fool you. I see all the "unnoticed" sins that everyone brushes under the rug as innocent, no big deal, and "everyone does it." I Am Truth, I honor My Father and you are called to walk by those standards. Are you honoring your Father with the lump of lies you've swept under the rug? Are you willing to roll away the rug and lets get those out of here? We need to deal with them one by one."

"What's swept under the rug most often? Daily sins that go unnoticed, bad habits that have become so routine you no longer notice them but are not of My Father? If you think about them, you will know them by name:"

"What are some of the sins from your past you haven't given over to Me, that maybe you thought We had just moved on from and We don't need to deal with since they are in the past? Well, it's time. I haven't forgotten them because you haven't given them to Me and asked for forgiveness. I Am not ashamed of you. I love you. There's no need to run from this place of truth and honesty. Confession brings life and hope to the dark places that used to keep you bound in fear and silent rejection of yourself. Honor Me by being real. Let's go to work. What cha got?"

"Now, I want you to honor yourself by giving Me the lies you have believed for so long. That you are never enough, that you won't measure up to those around you, that things will never change.....
The list goes on and on. But they all have one thing in common: they are all lies. Honor Me by listening to The Father of Truth, not the father of lies. He's taken enough space in your mind, lets deal with him once and for all."

VALIANT WARRIOR

"Mighty one,
Do not feel alone. I see your frustration and anger at the wrong that was done. I Am near. I Am working; do not give up hope. Call on Me in the times of worry, anger and regret. I never meant for you to go it alone. It is not strength when your efforts originate out of fear. Strength comes from seeking My face and drawing near to Me. Being still, hearing My voice telling you it's going to be ok. There are so many great things in store for you if have the faith to seek them. Look at things with a new set of eyes."

"Eyes of hope for change and opportunity to share My love and who I Am with you where you go. Your voice matters, many look to you for advice although you may not notice them. You cannot endure the things of this life without the fuel of My love. My strength will cover your weakness. Fear is not of Me, when you seek Me there's nothing to fear."

"The day comes, but you still fear Me. Why do you fear what you cannot "see?" I Am all around you and I Am good. Do not fear what you do not know. There is nothing to fear in Me, I Am for you. I go before you and prepare the way. When you walk in your flesh and try to pretend you don't know Me it only keeps Me away. I want us to be close. I want you to trust Me. Just because things seem hard and I *seem* distant doesn't mean that's the truth. Things are not always what they "seem." What is truth? I Am."

"I alone Am good. There's no evil in Me, My intentions or My will for your life. My soul purpose for your life is that you know Me as son and you trust Me as Father. I Am not like earthly fathers that can disappoint you or reject you. I Am The Good Father who sees your heart, your desires and wants you to trust in Me for all the things you ask. Trust in Me, I AM good."

VALIANT WARRIOR

"The night seems dark and intimidating because it seems to consume My light. My light pierces the darkness in your life when you let Me. I will never force you to ask for help, cause you to fear Me, but I do yearn for you to trust in Me. Trusting in Me, asking for My strength is never weakness it is wisdom. Darkness only feels intimidating because you feel out of control. All things are possible in My strength. What if instead of fear you choose trust? What if instead of anger you choose love? It won't make sense in the moment. It will not feel natural because this world is not of Me; it is run by the enemy. You must choose My way or his. If you choose nothing or do nothing you have still chosen. By not choosing to do what's right you are choosing to live by this world and what seems "logical", what feels good or what is easy."

"People choose what feels good or what's easy, choose to over look sins or choose to say no to what I ask because it takes effort to step out of your comfort zone. It takes effort to get over yourself long enough to listen or be there for someone who needs encouragement."

"I have called you by name for a purpose, your life matters to Me and the things I have called you to; I haven't forgotten I asked them of you. You are equipped and empowered by My Spirit to complete the calling I placed on your life. Do not fear your calling, I equip what I call. I won't leave you but it's up to you to trust and give Me control over your life. Are you ready to walk out your calling and lead others to Me?"

"You have to have the faith to believe I'm not settling and "having to" work with you but rather I have *intentionally created you the way you are* with gifts and talents that others need to hear Me and see Me. Those gifts are not an accident. It's not too late, you haven't missed it. Let's go. Take My hand let's go out into the darkness that is this world. Let's demonstrate who I Am and what I really stand for- all that is good, all that is Truth, honor and glory. Seek My face, My strength, lean on Me knowing I haven't and will never leave your side."

VALIANT WARRIOR

"You might feel alone or rejected –you are not alone and other people are not rejecting you, they are rejecting Me. I Am strong enough to handle it. Where do you feel Me leading you?"

"When you go out look for My lost ones. You will know them by their eyes and lack of the love of life in their words. Ask for words of encouragement and trust that I will provide the words they need. My Words speak life and Truth. My Words never fail and will be there when you ask."

"It takes courage to be bold enough to step outside your circumstance and comfort zone to be light to others. It's not hard once you just try. Step out in faith- I will not fail you. Go deeper than you are with Me now. Build your faith muscles in Me daily. If you are weak, it's because you haven't been feed yourself. You won't have the endurance to keep going or the energy to look for others to bless. You cannot give what you do not have. Time with Me in My Word and with Me in prayer is where you are fed to fight My war in love."

"There are few that are strong. Strength is as much mind endurance as it is physical stature. I Am not impressed by physical builds but by the heart in which is encased inside. Is your faith strong? Have you flexed your strength of faith to find out?"

"Many are weak because they don't exercise their faith. Faith is something that comes from trust. Believing in Me and My promises, but acting upon them without seeing the outcome before you start. Eventually you will get to a place where through the eyes of faith you <u>will</u> see the end result before you begin. This takes strong faith because the flesh which is of this world is weak. The flesh says if there's no immediate reward then it's not worth the effort. Strength that flows from the heart that's strong is brave. Brave because the natural world might call you crazy, mock and stop your plans. Seek My guidance along this path that your faith has you on. Ask to <u>see</u> the things I see, ask to be the things you need to be so you can be a blessing to those along your way in your faith journey."

VALIANT WARRIOR

"Living in fear causes people to make choices and actions from a place of insecurity and panic. Strong faith stands at the shore's edge, watches a large wave as it is barreling towards you and doesn't relent. In the moment of fear and trembling you seek My face and My strength and hold fast to your faith, planting your feet in deep knowing I Am with you and that this world, this adversity that is the wave will not overcome you. I Am stronger. This is where your faith is exercised. Seeing adversity headed your way, but instead of reacting and running in fear, you seek My strength and hold on in faith knowing My promise to never let this world be too much for you to bare. That's power. Knowledge of My strength. The power to hold on to My Words of Truth and life is the strongest form of faith there is."

"On the shore with your feet dug in deep, bravely embracing the oncoming wave you close your eyes trusting that I Am there, you suddenly see that what once looked so ominous is now a mere wash on your feet. The enemy is My footstool. When you have the faith and the eyes of strength to boldly face the things this world tries to scare you with and hold on, you will see they are merely a cleansing for the sand off your feet. Nothing is too hard for Me. Nothing is too much to ask of Me. It doesn't matter if the wave that is barreling at you was the result of your choices, when you seek Me and choose not to run and fear, that's when your strength and power, your faith is fully on display in My eyes. You open your eyes with a smile on your face, knowing I was with you in this place of fear, but your faith grew and now you stand on the shore looking out at the ocean full of waves, but you are no longer intimidated because you know I Am stronger."

"Your eyes of faith are now open. Use this vision of faith to see the unseen and walk out and stand firm in your faith in Me for all your circumstances. You will not only have a smile on your face when you are facing adversity but you will also be a light and a pillar of strength for others who are scared and want to run."

VALIANT WARRIOR

"Stay on the shore until you get it. Watch the waves roll in that become a mere whisper. When you are ready go out. Find others who are on the shore of their faith but have no idea what to do. When you share your story of vulnerability and faith when it seemed impossible that's when you are flexing your faith muscles. That's what impresses Me. When you seek Me, find Me, know and trust Me then you tell others your journey to help them along the way."

"Man has lost his voice in this generation. I made you the head of the household so you could hold firm and be the foundation for your family and generations to come. The man that seeks Me and has eyes to see things in faith builds the strongest household. The household needs a leader. Pick up your warriors heart I gave you to fight and go out in strength that comes from eyes of faith. Rebuild what has fallen in your family:
-Is it family time?
-Is it quality of relationships?
-Is it your own faith in Me?"

"Wherever you are, have the strength to ask for My help on the shore. Ask Me to fight for your family and restore it to what it was meant to be. But first you must start with My house which is your body. Our relationship-rebuild your temple where I reside. Remove the things that never belonged here like fear, rage, lust, competition and let My love overflow and purify your cup. You are the strength in My army, but the strength must come from a place of love, not war. Remember, the battle has already been won so you don't need to feel anxious, or react out of fear, but to <u>walk</u> in love, with eyes open to see those that are hurting and need to see what faith looks like *walked out*."

"What others choose to do with your love is not your responsibility. Each person must account for their own faith journey and relationship with Me. Be love, let go of those who refuse to see Me in you, who refuse to do what is right. People can let you down and leave you, but I will never fail you. I Am the only thing that is truly good and will never fail you."

"Don't fall for the snare the enemy entangles you with on the shore that is bitterness, resentment, rage and rejection. Be strong knowing you hear My voice. You have sought Me and now you know Me. I stand out and Am easily found with the eyes of faith you see with now. My strength is enough for the both of us. Lets move on from strength and move to the heart."

"Where's your faith? Your faith comes from the things you believe in. Do you believe in the things you have been able to achieve with your own hands, conversations and abilities or is your faith in knowing I will provide for you? I qualify the called. The called are qualified by their faith in Me. Faith to step out in fear because it's not in your strength, abilities that you move forward but in following My voice that says "Come, see, taste, know that I Am good." There's so much more to this life than earthly riches and possessions, selfie status and fame. When you see The Kingdom all these things will no longer seem important."

"The thing that is important is knowing who your <u>heart</u> says I Am. Who do you say I Am? Not who Peter said I was, but who do <u>you</u> say I Am? Am I <u>The</u> Christ? Am I your Savior or am I just your bail bondsman- getting you out of the chains you like to keep putting on? There's a difference between the two. One leads to an eternal life of freedom and the other only gives freedom from a circumstance. Are you tired of the game? Are you ready to trust Me with all of your life instead of just your circumstances? What if we walked together in this life but in My strength instead of yours? What if you trusted Me as Lord and Savior instead of exterminator of issues that irritate you like a buzzing mosquito? When you only allow Me access to little things in your life- life circumstances, that's all you get. A life without "mosquitoes." If someone offered you a vast kingdom with never ending happiness, joy, peace and love would you take it? That's what I Am. I Am the Savior and King over this Kingdom. This Kingdom belongs to My Father. It is freely offered, but to enter here you must offer up earthly things, your sinful life, thoughts, and actions, allow Me to wash your entire life, not just your current circumstances. Give all of it to Me and all of it will be made new. Do not fear the unknown. I will never leave your side. With this surrender comes a new life. A new beginning, a new way of thinking. Where others become your focus instead of an inward thought life; you begin to see the hurting, lost and afraid. You become My light bearer for them to see Me. You become My strength in flesh because you have surrendered to My will for your life not yours."

"I Am not a dictating ruler who is controlling- I Am Father and friend who seeks companionship and a faithful heart to remain loyal to. I Am not here to control but to comfort you. I Am not here to condemn but to love. I did not die for you to live a life full of "things" but for the love of The Father and peace in this joy that is the outpouring of His love. Few are strong enough to fully surrender because this life says surrender is weak."

"But surrender to The Father is wise and strong because a surrendered heart becomes pliable and I Am allowed to become your armor you wear. You are protected because you are clothed in My righteousness, My holiness and My goodness. You no longer fear circumstances and people because they cannot overcome you. I Am with you-there's no need to ever fear when you are clothed in My love and righteousness. My armor bearer is a mighty warrior in My sight because He was willing to take up this cross, let down his pride and seek Me wholeheartedly. Can you hear them? The army of The Lord in the distance. Are you ready to join them in this fight? They are calling you to join them. This battle is not like earthly battles that tear at the flesh by seeking dominion and reign over someone. This battle starts from a submissive heart to The Father's will, a mind that has been transformed by love and faith in the One that has called you son."

"My sons fight for My honor in this battle. This battle is won by prayers and love not swords of the tongue. Pray for those who are blind and have not yet found Me. Pray for those who have chosen to reject Me. Pray for those who have no fight left."

VALIANT WARRIOR

Love. Love is My greatest weapon. When you love your enemy they are confused because no one has loved them before-especially someone who has intentionally tried to cause harm. Love them sincerely- not as a means of revenge but truly love and pray for them. Watch the spear that pierces their heart. It's their weakness. My love pierces the most guarded of hearts."

"Never miss-use My Father's love for your own gain, pride or arrogance. Love of The Father is genuine and not self-seeking glory, fame, and revenge. I Am love, My warriors fight in My armor I clothe you in and fight for My Father's honor not theirs. When the battle lines are drawn will you stand and fight in My Father's name or will you raise your own banner and try to protect your own honor?"

"Hear the words I speak of truth and life. You are not alone in this place. I have known you from the beginning and will be with you always. You draw strength from Me when its convenient but you rely on your own strength more. What if you sought Me first? What if My words sent you out each day? What if you sought My counsel instead of the counsel of man? Man is limited and has flaws. I AM omnipotent and omnipresent and have never had a flaw. The Alpha and Omega has spoken the beginning into existence and knows the end of man's time here until My Kingdom comes to the new earth. When you seek My counsel and My will there are no mistakes because I Am guiding you in all that is good. Go to the place I will show you, gather the lost to Me. When you go out clothe yourself in My peace and love. Do not fear rejection and loosing your way. I Am with you and preparing the hearts of those along the way."

"It's difficult for man to truly love. Man guards his heart as though it's his job to protect it. Vulnerability and honesty leads best to those seeking the lost. If you seek the lost with an agenda built on the foundation of pride, it will be obvious that they are your "project" and not the object of My devotion."

VALIANT WARRIOR

"Vulnerability and transparency of My love on display makes the most headway in The Kingdom. You cannot "achieve" people into The Kingdom for your namesake. You must clothe yourself in love, righteousness and humility seeking to be a blessing to those who feel there is no hope. Not waiting to hear back from them that you were a blessing, this is your gain and not My Father's gain. Go out in My name for My Father's Kingdom, not to grow a Kingdom of fans in your name. Those who prostrate themselves before Me will be greatest."

"Draw to Me when you feel alone. I know the desires of your heart and how you feel like you have been abandoned at times, like you are not seen or heard. Men feel alone too; it's not strange or weak. You feel alone when you *don't realize* I never leave your side."

"Seek Me first and My righteousness and all things will be added to you. I have called you by name for your purpose only you can fulfill. I Am El Roi- "The God who Sees." I never miss a thing. I see your lost heart and desires for change. I see your hope and hopelessness. Nothing goes unnoticed. I hear the cries of your heart, I know the thoughts you have – good and bad. I love you just the same. I Am The Good Father that has never and will never leave your side. Have faith in My Words, have faith in My Truth which is My love for you that is never ending."

"The time is here. Draw near to Me. Not the way you are accustomed to but in My way. My way requires obedience to the ways I Am. Obedience is a choice. You can choose to live in the way in which I direct your path or you can choose to live in obedience to your flesh. People don't like the word "obedience" because they think it demoralizes them somehow. Obedience to The Father shows a commitment and full-blown faith. Obedience is not mindless following but an act of love. Because I first loved you and sought you, now you should do the same."

VALIANT WARRIOR

"Love the things I love, honor The Father the way I honor The Father. Choose to live by His precepts. Forgive those who have persecuted you. Yes, even that person. Forgiveness doesn't remove what they have done wrong but it removes the stronghold in your heart the enemy uses to keep your heart from Me fully."

"Honor your Father and Mother. If your parents are still here on earth, have you honored them in the way you should of? Do you owe them a debt? Do you owe them an apology? Have you served them the way they served you when you were a child? If your parents are the ones you have to forgive- it's time. Honor them because I ask you to and forgive them. I Am The Good Father that will never fail you. When you honor your parents you are honoring your heavenly Father."

"Are you loving your neighbor as yourself? Not polite small talk and pleasantries, but actually loving your neighbor as yourself? What do you wish someone would do for you? Go do it for them. Take a burden off someone's shoulders instead of heaping more workload onto them, take some off of them. Seek out The Kingdom of God here on earth. Be love, show them Me. Be The Father's heart in the way you love when the flesh says *be impatient, get revenge,*" or call on someone who owes you something."

"Look with the eyes of The Father everywhere you go- seeking for someone who needs to know I love them. Show them love; show them what it means to be a "son" of God. You must first know what that truly means before you can show someone what that means. What does that mean for you? Just that you are "saved?", that you will live eternally here in heaven with Us? That's only a portion of your inheritance. Would you like to see your inheritance? Look outside at night. Can you count My stars? I know all their names. There are more stars than what your eyes can see. Now, go look on the internet to see the vast galaxies I spoke into existence. Just like the stars and galaxies, there's no limit to what My love means. There's no limit to the things The Father can provide."

VALIANT WARRIOR

"My love for you was paid for by My love for you on the cross. Your debt was washed away when I clothed myself in your sin. When My death and resurrection was complete your sin debt was paid. The enemy makes you feel like you are not worthy of your inheritance. You feel like you are not good enough because of the things you think, choose to do or not to do. All lies. My love is unconditional. Believe that I, Jesus Christ died on the cross for your sins, rose again and Am seated at the right hand of The Father and you are saved."

"Nothing more. There's no "work" required to pay me back. I do ask that you show them The Father's love by loving you the way I love you. Love when love doesn't make sense. Choose obedience to The Father and show them His heart. See where The Father takes you."

"A man has a special place in My heart. He is that pillar of strength that holds a household in union. You are called to lead by example, show them Me, loving like I love you. If you don't know Me and My love for you, how will you show them? Ask Me who I Am, Ask Me to open your eyes and ears to the Truth which is the Word. Seek more of Me. Seek Me first in your day. Seek Me in all things. I'm not just in your church building. You don't need to wait to get to the building to spend time with Me. I Am everywhere. Talk to Me, ask to find Me and I will show you more of Me. I have sought you out from the beginning and am wanting more of you when you are ready to know Me more. Don't fear Me, I Am good."

"The things of this life won't last forever. I Am the only thing that remains. I was and always will be. When you join Me in faith you will walk with Me just like it was in the beginning. I seek companionship and friendship with My children. All are sons and daughters but not all accept My love and My offer of salvation and must be separated from Me. I know the hearts of man and the desires for evil is why My grace of My blood was shed."

"You cannot denounce or ignore sins and desires that are not of Me. You must realize they are there, confess them and ask Me to wash you clean again. I make all things new. My love for My sons and daughters doesn't change. I have loved you from the beginning and My love never fails or leaves because of the actions or thoughts of man."

"I Am The Alpha and Omega- the beginning and the end. Authority to judge was given to Me by My Father and therefore I must judge the sins and actions of man. My judgment of man doesn't change My love of man. My heart grieves and My soul yearns for compete surrender to The Father's will in your life, but not all people are willing to put the desires of the flesh aside for The Creator, author and finisher of all life."

"There is no striving for My love. My love is eternal. It is never ending and unfailing. Period. What you do in My name doesn't make Me love you more than I already do. You don't need to prove your love to Me. I know you love Me. I know your heart and your inner most thoughts and intentions. I Am El Roi, The God that Sees. I see all things. Inward and outward, nothing is hidden from My sight. This shouldn't intimidate you this should call you to a higher place. A place that is no longer about "doing" but being."

"Seek Me first. Seek The Father's Kingdom. Seek to love the least and the lost. Don't fear I don't know your love for Me or that you haven't "shown" Me how much you love Me by your actions. My love is different than your capacity to love. I AM perfect. You will be made perfect when you are glorified in My presence. I don't think of you less, love you less because of your "failures" or "imperfections." I know you had them and would have them from the beginning. I formed you and chose you anyway. This shouldn't sadden you like I have to "settle" for you. I love you. You are My treasured possession. A Father guides and teaches His children and that's what I Am here for. You must not think I Am disappointed. I want a sincere heart, a repentant heart and a heart for The Father and I will do the rest."

VALIANT WARRIOR

"Join Me. My army of believers, seeking and searching the hearts of the lost. All it takes is a heart that is willing. Are you willing? If the answer is yes, you must first know your role. I Am Savior. It is not your obligation to try and "save" someone. Many have gone before you that had this concept twisted. Pride has a way of hiding in "good works." I alone Am Savior. Now that you know it's not your job but Mine that should make things a lot easier for you-more peaceful and not such a daunting task."

"Next, Am I your Savior? You can't tell other people about Me if I Am not Lord and Savior over your life. What are you keeping from Me? The things you think are too small and insignificant for Me to "worry" about. All things are easy for Me, don't believe the lie that something is too small and you shouldn't "bother" Me with it. So, what are they?"

"Are you strong enough to give them to Me? What would your life look like if you gave Me your burdens? All of them. I Am ready and I Am willing."

VALIANT WARRIOR

"My warriors must not only call Me Lord and Savior, but must also be fed well. Fed on My Word- it is the only thing that satisfies spiritual hunger. Have you sought Me in My pages? Are you asking for things to be revealed to you so that you will know My heart for you and all of My people?"

"My Word is not meant to be viewed as a task, accomplishment or something only to be done on Sundays. It's fellowship with Me and knowing My heart for you. I created you with fellowship in mind. Not to rule over you as a dictatorship but as a Father and friend. Don't be afraid to let Me in as those roles in your life. I Am good. You can trust in Me. I see your heart and the fear you keep inside. On the outside you are brave and strong but on the inside you fear your whole world will crumble. I Am trustworthy with your world. Are you willing to let Me into your secret place where there are no secrets between the two of us? A place without shame, regret, anger or doubt? I can make all things new. When you surrender all these things to Me, I can make them new. It's time. What are you willing to surrender?"

VALIANT WARRIOR

"Days have gone by, you have thought about our conversation, but thought I wasn't talking about you. Well, I Am. I Am interested in you. Being omnipresent there's nothing that can take Me from you. You are not keeping Me from someone else who "needs" Me more. Well? Are you willing? What do you want Me to know?"

"It takes courage to be vulnerable. You grow the most when you expose things as though I didn't already know. You give them to Me as a sign of trust. I Am working in these areas that have scarred your past. Your past doesn't define you. I do. You are My son, whom I love and Am well pleased. When I hung on the cross and even before the foundation of the world, I knew these things and yet you didn't disappoint Me. I understand human weakness. It's time you understand grace. My grace is enough for you. Punishing yourself is works of the flesh trying to earn forgiveness. My death on the cross paid for all sin. Stop trying to belittle My work that was finished in Calvary."

VALIANT WARRIOR

"It's a new day. Don't be afraid to hope for the promises of the future. When you fear the future it reveals your lack of faith that I Am for you and that I Am good. What are you not trusting Me for, the deepest thoughts, "smallest" of dreams that seem so insignificant?"

"Share your heart- I AM Father, The Creator, The Author and The Finisher. The more vulnerable and honest you are the closer we are able to grow."

VALIANT WARRIOR

"Hearts are heavy when they carry burdens I never asked you to bare. When you walk around with shame and guilt around your ankles they are like shackles that trip you up, cause you not to run- they set boundaries for what you can do and the pace at which you do them because you know they limit you and remind you of your past mistakes."

"I have the key. Do you want them off? For some reason you have made them part of who you are as though you are not worthy of complete freedom. Pride makes you feel this."

"It's pride hidden behind the mask of humiliation. You think this is who you are and you want to feel limited, as though chained and bound by regrets, fear, anger, and mistakes can prevent you from your calling. It's not "your" calling. My calling for you, I spoke over you. My calling over you doesn't include limits or restraints. It's up to you to ask to be free."

"Did that sink in or did you just move on like usual? Some of you reading this chose freedom and now you feel the release and weightlessness I have been calling you to. Others of you reading this think I was talking about someone else and your issues/shackles are not what I was talking about. Nope. That was you too. Lets stand here and look at them. Look Me in the eye. Are you ready for freedom? Why do you fear trusting Me to let you out? Are you afraid that I Am not who I say I Am? I already know the future and the outcome of what you will choose. I'm just letting you catch up. I love you and I Am. There is nothing I lack or fear. Even your rejection of My love and freedom I have promised you. True bravery comes from putting your faith in the unknown you have not given to Me yet. Come. Allow Me to lead you, allow Me to set you free. I Am good. I Am The I Am."

VALIANT WARRIOR

"I Am Here- in the stillness you call prison. Stillness is not a prison unless you are unhappy with the company you keep. Why do you hate to be alone with Me- why do you fear the things I want to say? I Am good. I Am not a tyrant. I am not a mean dictator wanting to punish you for your rebellion and rejection of Me. I Am good. I alone. You know Me but only allow Me into certain aspects of your life. I Am not going to ask you to give up the things you love -the things that are pure and good I planted in your heart. That's why you love what you love. I wouldn't take away the seed of joy I panted in your heart. You alone can unlock this cage you isolate yourself in. I can come in and cause this cage to return to dust with a word, but I will not force Myself on you- it is you who must invite Me into this place of desolation in your heart. I will wait."

VALIANT WARRIOR

"Hear the truth in My voice and feel the peace of My presence. There is nothing better than My dwelling place. This is the ultimate treasure and riches a man can possess. All other things <u>will</u> fade away. I have always been and will be. My character never changes. I Am all that is pure and holy, just and mighty yet I chose to seek the heart of everyone, it is your choice to notice and accept Me. Are you ready to experience more of Me? Do you even want Me in your day-to-day life?"

"Money and wealth are bait on fishing line that is on dry land. You run, struggle and grovel trying to obtain it but when you exert yourself and humiliate yourself in desperation to obtain it, it is snatched out of your hands quickly and there's nothing to show for your efforts except exhaustion and frustration. Are you willing to walk past this trap? Have you struggled long enough? Are you willing to see money/wealth for what it is? It is a useful tool, <u>not</u> a destination or identity. Money is great if used wisely. Money is intoxicating because it tempts you to do things to obtain more of it. See the line the enemy has baited you with? When it's your only focus you end up exhausted, angry and still without wealth. Stand beside the money and at the end of the line. See past the game you have fallen for all of your life. Money doesn't define you. I do."

"It's ok to have money, but it's not ok for it to be your obsession and to exhaust yourself for something that is fleeting. Ask for My favor. Take your eyes off this money on the baited line. Seek Me more than ever before and you will have wealth that only comes from walking with Me in My presence. I Am all you need. I know the needs that you have tried to obtain money to buy. I can provide for you and give you joy and peace because you are in My presence. Dare to trust Me."

VALIANT WARRIOR

"Danger can be real or can be in the mind. The mind is a harbor for both good and bad things if you let it. Harboring guilt, harboring lust, harboring regret, harboring shame, and harboring the things that someone said in the past. All this clouds your mind and makes it like a fog. You cannot sail where you have been called to go in a mental fog. Strangely enough mental fogs are often a comfort zone. It has the ability to hold you like a prisoner and keep you in a place you were never meant to stay. Your decking can mildew your boat can collect barnacles and rust. Because of the fog you aren't even aware that things are starting to fall away. What have you been harboring that you need to lift?"

"Are you ready to face the truth and not fear the things I have called you to in this life? Are you ready to forgive those who have hurt and disappointed you in the past? They have been the one tethering you to the dock. Bound mentally and holding you from going forward. You no longer need to fear the sail. I never asked you to be a prisoner of your regrets. The real danger is admitting that the mental fog of regret, resentment and worry exists and refuse to untie the rope at the dock to sail out. Sail away from what seems safe, secure, what you have known."

"Just because it's what you have known doesn't mean that's where you are meant to stay. Allow Me to untie the rope and guide you to the place you are meant to be. Free from guilt, shame, regret, and doubt of your calling. Your life is not meant to just exist. I called you to a life. Are you living? Are you willing to forgive, move on and love yourself- you can't keep these weights of the anchor of shame and sail where I Am calling you."

VALIANT WARRIOR

"Out on the water you have a view of things to come. Things don't seem uncertain, unfamiliar but rather intriguing and inviting. You were meant to explore unencumbered. Look out onto the horizon. What have you been afraid to go after? Is it to satisfy an earthly gain that someone told you that you "needed" that will only leave you empty again? What if instead you sought My face? I Am near, I Am all-powerful. Seeking My face takes courage and strength. Laying down the things of this life is even harder. It seems like you are "giving up" things to satisfy Me but actually you are giving up things that will never satisfy you."

"I see all things, I know all things, My desire for you is to walk in your calling, to know where you were meant to sail and thrive here. This place is not always going to be smooth and calm waters. Storms will arise, but because you had the courage to seek My face and to seek Me first you will not be unprepared."

"Where's your faith? Are you strong enough to do this for real? Not just explore the thought in your mind, but actually do it this time? Before we go lets talk about the fog you have allowed to cloud your view of your calling:

-Unrest in your heart- fear you will not be able to provide for the needs of your family.

-Pride and arrogance of your gain- success is not success if you are patting yourself on the back. Who's cheering you on? Is it The Father or the fair weather friend?

-Temper of resentment- do you respond to people in an unhealthy way because you are feeling like you haven't been honored? Honor will come naturally or won't come at all, sometimes even when it might be deserved. Your anger is a gage that shows weakness in your heart. There's a place hidden deep within that makes you crave value from man. Man does not determine your worth, I do. Do you know that I have called you son? I have called you by name for a specific purpose that will fulfill the deepest places of your heart. The first step to finding your calling is to be still."

VALIANT WARRIOR

"Ask to see My face. Not as a stranger confronts a stranger with a stance of defense but as a son greets his father or a friend meets up with a friend he hasn't seen in years. That's the joy in which I want you to seek Me. I never leave your side, yet you choose to go through this life without asking for My wisdom and strength as though it was bothersome or weak. You are not a helpless child going back home to dad because some bully in the yard made you scared. When you seek Me, we war together. I Am your shield, I Am your strength. We war together in the things that battle for your mind. It takes courage to seek Me instead of running."

"Are you ready? Can I loosen the straps at the dock? Are you ready for freedom and life of abundance? Draw near to Me, seek My face ask for My strength and direction. Forgive those you need to forgive- forgive yourself for the regrets of the past. Watch the fog lift and hope arise. There's nothing uncertain when you seek My will first. I see all things including your heart. You yearn to know Me more, but until now you have been afraid. Keep being who you are, the man you have become, but now you won't be blinded by the fog of regret and fear; and will have a hope for things to come."

VALIANT WARRIOR

"All kingdoms belong to Me. Although earthly kingdoms have many rulers, there is only one Heavenly Kingdom. This is the Kingdom that matters. Although man has been granted authority over earthly kingdoms and satan has been given limited authority over these principalities-ultimately The I Am rules."

"I use all things for My good. Even the evil in the hearts of man gets used by My Father for His glory. I Am not bound by the limits of man's thoughts or actions. I can speak things into existence from nothing. Why fear the man who is ruler over your earthly kingdom? Why let satan walk in your dwelling place of your mind and give him the keys to the things you fear? His power is limited and only has dominion over the things you give him the keys to. There are weaknesses in your mind so unguarded you don't even have a gate to keep him out. He has been in this place so long, you thought he belonged and was just a part of life you had to deal with. You have believed the lie he played for you. You have given him free reign over this place and have become his slave."

"I came to break the bondage of failure, regret, weakness, sorrow and even death. Kick out the defeated liar that has ruled over your mind's kingdom for so long. You appointed him; now its time you fire him. Fire him in My name. The name above all names, the name that has the only true authority over all life and even over death."

"Now that your mind has become vacant and lost its "ruler" you need to appoint Me as guardian and ruler over your mind and body. Are you willing to let Me into this place where I AM truly Lord over your life?"

VALIANT WARRIOR

"Days seem long; things seem tiring and un-ending at times. There's nothing to fear even when you don't see things happening. I Am in all things- the things visible and in the un-seen. When you look for a sign, you can feel empty and like I Am not for you. I Am always for you. I knew you before you knew Me. Give Me your burdens, give Me your desires for a better future, for a better now."

"There's nothing impossible for Me and there's nothing so small that you shouldn't ask. Allow Me to be in your thoughts and every breath you breathe. When you feel your breath- that's how you know I'm watching over you and working on your behalf. I never stop My love for you. Even when you disappoint Me and yourself, My love for you never changes. Take courage, be brave. This world needs a man of honor and valor."

"Honor comes when you honor those who don't normally get or "earn" honor. Honor comes when your flesh doesn't "feel" like it but you choose to say what you would want someone to say to you. Do they have qualities or characteristics you admire? Ask for mentoring; let them know you admire them for things you admire. Most men are so busy thinking they are not enough that they don't ever feel like they are honorable much less often think to honor someone else. What if it started with you? What if you lead the charge and you were first of your friends-<u>MEN</u> of VALOR that honored and built each other up as warriors of God?"

"Imagine strapping on warrior gear and going into battle- a man fought for you on the field- would you tell him that you appreciate his fight? That's the tone and way you should war for each other. Everyday is a battle. My people are in a battlefield for souls. If My men of valor are defeated and too weak to build each other up- the enemy is already winning."

"Can you take the victory on the field? Can you fight with each other as My warriors instead of being so single minded and only concerned about your "world?" Just because you can't see the war, if you listen you can hear the warriors in heaven chanting and cheering you on."

VALIANT WARRIOR

"Have you been under the Friday Night Lights? Have you felt the excitement of what could be? Have you felt what it feels like to prepare, run the plays and work together to accomplish the goal- warring for the win? If you weren't on the field you have been in a place where you felt like you were warring with them. You secretly wished you were out there fighting too. You just haven't noticed <u>you are</u> on the field. Close your eyes. Can you feel the beat of the drums? Can you feel your heart beating faster in excitement? The battle is now, the time is now and the way the battle is won is with My love. It's a battle to bring hope and courage to the men that need it. Champion the warrior that has been resting within."

VALIANT WARRIOR

"Man of My Word- you take My Words spoken by My mouthpieces so long ago and use them as your shield of righteousness. My Words are truth, life and protection when you know them. Do you feel their presence? Can you feel the protective barrier My Words provide? They are weapons of warfare for all who oppose you. Use them in defense and offense… My Words are used in defense to protect My Father and His character as well as My Son, whom I love. You are My son, I have called you by name and you are a mighty warrior. My Words are in your quill box and are sharp arrows. These arrows are not meant to tear people down. Don't use them from a place of fear, but as a source of confidence that nothing out-matches the Truth that is My Word."

"Stand tall and confident knowing you have My Word as your shield of righteousness; they are mighty when applied to your bow and pierce into the hearts of man. My Word should never be used to justify something for your gain or value but rather to bring My Father's righteousness into light."

"My Word comes from My Father's heart. My Father's heart is not insecure, looking to "shoot" people with Truth to prove He's stronger. I Am Truth and there's no one mightier. Imagine a huge warrior dressed in battle gear sitting down in a field holding a child back by the forehead. Although the child is swinging, kicking and shows great determination, the warrior is only tolerating him for a while. The "child-like" enemy may kick your shins and cause aggravation because he's persistent, but there's no need to feel threatened. You are that huge warrior & he's no match for the Word of My Truth. There's times when My Words can be spoken in a gentle voice to calm the scared attacker and there's times when My Word becomes a mighty arrow to pierce an enemy and bring an end to his game. Mighty warriors in My Father's name know when to use the tools He provides."

VALIANT WARRIOR

"Confidence is knowing you have these weapons and that they are available when you need them. Confidence comes from knowing you don't need to tell people you have them. Confidence is also not needing to tell them that you are strong and mighty. When you seek Me first and know your place in My Father's house and the position He's placed you here on the battlefield, there's no need to defend yourself- only My Father's honor."

"Imagine yourself as a mighty warrior, built from years of your work you put into developing your muscles and strength. Your confidence you have from the years of experience with your commander training you in the ways of war. This little child that comes at you is no match. Do not loose this image of yourself, if that's who you are- a mighty warrior."

"Have you eagerly sought My face? Have your sought My Father's will? Are you willing to know Me personally instead of through someone else? You can't assume the title of warrior in My army if you haven't developed the muscle in the gym that is quiet time with Me. When you seek Me first and My Father's will for your life and use what you learn about Me from My Word and from our time together, this is what develops you into My strong warrior, cut and built for anything that tries to attack you or your mind."

"You can't just show up to the battlefield with another man's quiet time and things he's learned about Me. Just like you wouldn't try to live your day on a meal someone else ate."

"So many people are confused why they are weak but it's because they have fallen for the lie of believing that the crumbs from The Father's table are all they are valuable enough to receive. I have called you to sit at this table with Me at the banquet prepared for My Father. You are not called to grovel on the ground for scraps and think this is where you belong. Take My hand and sit in this seat that is ready for you to occupy. This place is a place of great fellowship and comradery because everyone knows their worth that is defined by The Father's love alone."

"There will be times when My Word becomes an arrow to pierce the lies of the enemy but when you seek Me first, you will hear My voice and know if this is an actual threat or just a little kid kicking and screaming and you. You only need to talk softly to him from the place of confidence as the man your Father has called you."

"Time with Me should never be a place of burden or frustration. It should be like eating honeycomb in the desert. This world is like a desert; it has many harsh conditions that cause you to feel stressed and weak. When you seek Me first and you ask Holy Spirit to feed you on My Word, it's like honeycomb- so sweet and satisfying. My Truth written is nourishment for your soul. The Holy Spirit will reveal to you the inner meanings and teach you its applications. Ask Him to open your eyes to these Truths before you read. Repent and remove all impure thoughts that you allow in your mind. When you confess the things hidden in your heart, it renews your soil of your heart and allows My Word to settle into a new and fertile place where it can take root and become a bountiful harvest."

"Sharpen your arrows and pull back your bow. It's time to go into battle. You are not alone in this war fueled by love. My Father's love for the lost burns within your bones and yearns to reach those who don't know Me. Run out into the wilderness that is your sphere of influence. Unlike a fight to devour, this a fight for love- The love of The Father. The arrows are not meant to destroy people, but to deliver deliverance. The arrows pierce the hearts and minds of those who have been in bondage for too long."

"They yearn to be free, seek a new way of living. Their arms burn from the chains that bind their wrists of their mind. They run out each day but are pulled back because they are tethered to the same mentality- a defeated mindset."

"The arrows are freedom for the men you know. They are keys to freedom when you use them correctly. They unlock the chains and bring forth victory when you know where to aim. You cannot approach in a mindset of pride or arrogance but of a prison guard. You have seen them in bondage for years and thought they would never escape but now you realize you have the keys to allow them to find Me- their freedom."

"This prison has been self-imposed for many men. Seeking wealth, status and monetary gain they bound themselves here unintentionally. While they inhabited this cell, their mindset became complacent- they have settled into this as if *"this is all there is and I am going to make the best of it."* They have forgotten their calling and the man their Father has called them to be. Some were born here from their previous generations deliverance here. Placed here from their earthly father's choices and lack of seeking Me. Some arrived here by choice- deliberately running from Me with a defiant mind- a mindset that "control" in a prison is better than freedom under My rule."

"They have misunderstood My love and thought of Me as a dictating and ruling judge who condemns those who reject Me out of scorn and hate. I actually mourn for all that reject My love. It's their choice to reject Me that separates us. I yearn to know them all as close companions, but they have listened to the lies about Me. That's where your arrows come in. These arrows are powerful and full of My love. The quill is My Father's hand guiding it to the depth of their heart."

"How you reach them is by asking to Holy Spirit to reveal the deepest desire of their heart to you and pray that over them. Your friendship with them has given you access to My lost sons bound from Me. Go to them in love, pray for words of knowledge, pray for favor when you speak to them, pray they hear the love of The Father in your voice. Just as a warrior suits up for battle- he knows what he's up against- you too must realize the war you are fighting."

"Many men don't realize they are in bondage; many men like the bondage and some are even punishing themselves thinking this is where they belong. No one belongs in bondage. Are you ready to fight for them? Can you go to them with a humble heart, one that seeks to break My captives free? Love breaks all bonds- no matter how much scarring has taken place."

VALIANT WARRIOR

"I Am healer and Am eternal life. Do not fear you are unequipped. I walk beside those who seek Me. I exalt the lowly and strengthen the weary."

"There's a reason you were chosen to read these pages- you are called to reach My lost sons. Even the sons who have found Me and know Me as Lord and Savior, but still haven't released control of their minds and life to Me."

"When you freely give all that is yours, that's where true freedom is found. My limitless resources, My strength, courage, commitment and character. Your calling is great. Just because you don't feel qualified doesn't mean I haven't called you. My love for you is beckoning you to reach those I love."

"Do you hear My voice, have you sought My face? Do you rely on Me more than you rely on yourself? Why do you insist on being "brave" and trying to "exist" in your own strength? Would you rather view yourself in the armor I clothed you in or would you rather continue on the familiar path- wondering what the day will bring? Look in the mirror. I created you – a man of deep faith, character and internal strength. You have sought Me, but now its time to submit to Me."

"There's a difference between seeking and submitting. Submitting means you trust your commander- The Lord of this army that seeks the lost. All My men are enlisted here but it's not always evident. They wonder around aimlessly because they didn't ask for their calling. Your calling is to enlist. Enlist in the depth of My love. Fully embrace and take on the depth of this place."

"My love for you knows no limits. My scars on the cross bore My love for you. When you hear My voice in the stillness go there in your mind- ask to see Me. I never leave your side and I Am warring along with you. You never should feel alone. Here's what I see when I look at you- valor. Many don't understand what it means to be a man of valor- it means you are unshaken because your foundation is firm. It's a place of strength because you know who you are."

VALIANT WARRIOR

"Man of Valor-
I have called you by name. You have been given a great purpose in this life. Your purpose is to seek Me first in <u>all</u> things. To take in The Father's love like a quenching rain. Let it penetrate your inner core until you have become saturated by My love. When you are fully saturated you will naturally over flow My love into your life and into those around you."

"My love comforts and condemns. Condemnation comes to those who need to repent of things that separate us. Things that are not of Me are not ok in you. Condemnation is not a life of guilt, but a gate of redemption. When you ask for forgiveness of your sins, those sins are washed away in The Father's love. This world's ruler has made condemnation a bad word. He has clothed it in guilt and chains. My condemnation is a chance for freedom. Give it to Me; ask for forgiveness and it's gone. No guilt, no shame only closeness to The Father. Your confession releases you from any guilt or shame the enemy tries to throw at you like mud."

"I wash away all things that don't belong in you. When you accept Me as Lord and Savior your eternal chains of condemnation are no more. The enemy makes you think any failures, sins and mistakes define you as a man. My Father defines you as "son." Have you accepted this title? You cannot earn this title. It is freely given to those who seek Me and My Father's love. I sit at the right hand and rule, but I also walk beside those who seek Me. Dare to know Me like never before. Are you willing to see where your faith will take you?"

"Suit up. Wake up early and look out over the horizon –where do you feel your battleground is? Can you see them? Can you hear them crying out for freedom? This battle cannot be won in human strength, only out of Mine. You are not fighting an earthly fight but a fight in the spiritual realm- a fight for lost souls. A fight for freedom of those who are sons locked in habitual chains of traditions and tendencies."

VALIANT WARRIOR

"Seek Me first; this is where your strength comes from. Seek Me and listen for instructions on who needs to know My love today. You might be given an image of someone to pray for; you might notice someone in your normal daily routine that needs a word of encouragement. Don't dismiss the mundane and routine of life as though you are not "in battle." Battles are where you walk. They occur in the minds of all My sons and daughters. They put on a front as though they fine but deep down a war is raging. You have the keys to freedom to redeem the lost. The ones troubled by this life, the ones depressed because they haven't found their way. The ones who are puffed up in pride "thinking" they are ok but have no clue they are bound."

"Love of The Father must be your fuel that drives you. You are not earning My love and respect. I already love you and you are My son. Walk with Me to this mountaintop and tell Me what you see- off in the distant land there's a faint cry. You can hear them when you use your spiritual ears to hear them. Many are waiting for a sign. Their sign has been right beside them all along. Their sign could be in their check out line at the grocery store. Wherever you go-look into the eyes of My people, ask Me to speak to their hearts through you and I will deliver what they yearn for."

"Don't fall for the lie of "not being able to hear Me" because you do hear Me. I Am here and I won't ever let you down. Don't fall for the lie of rejection. Few are willing to go into battle for The Father. When someone comes in My Father's name it's not always well received. They have a life of bitterness that causes them to reject Me because of man's manipulation of Me for their gain. Those men sought approval, value and worth from man not My Father's will. It has jaded many men from knowing Me."

"Don't give up. You are mighty. When they make a face or say words that dismiss or reject what you have said, that doesn't remove the arrow you placed. Arrows placed in love stay put and deliver a message that will penetrate their hearts and minds. Just because you don't see an immediate or favorable response doesn't mean you missed or that you failed. Your calling is to love; your calling is to seek My hurting and broken men- to tell them their true identity that is only found in Me."

VALIANT WARRIOR

"When you war in love, no shot arrow is ever wasted. My warriors are not prideful but powerful. They are powerful when they submit to My Father's command. Love is the only arrow that defeats lies of the enemy which leads to bondage."

"Now, from on top of this mountain look beside you- can you see them? Each of My warriors who war along side of you. Go out as a multitude that shapes this earth in My Father's love. Unite as men of valor together. Do not compete for titles or attention. Minister to each other, stand firm in their place when they are weak. Lend a helping hand when they are knocked down by the things of this life. You are not alone. You are a mighty army of love."